WOMEN OF THE AFRICAN ARK

A BOOK OF POSTCARDS

Photographs by
CAROL BECKWITH
and ANGELA FISHER

Pomegranate Artbooks / San Francisco

Pomegranate Artbooks
Box 6099
Rohnert Park, CA 94927

Pomegranate Europe Ltd.
Fullbridge House, Fullbridge
Maldon, Essex CM9 7LE
England

ISBN 1-56640-611-0
Pomegranate Catalog No. A696

Pomegranate publishes books of
postcards on a wide range of subjects.
Please write to the publisher for more information.

Printed in Korea
05 04 03 02 01 00 99 98 97 96 15 14 13 12 11 10 9 8 7 6

THE REGION OF ETHIOPIA and its surrounding countries—the Horn of Africa—is known today as a land of famine and war, but it is also the last secret kingdom of the world, a land of mystery and fierce beauty. Cut off by soaring mountain ranges, burning lava deserts, unexplored wildernesses and an isolated Indian Ocean coastline, the Horn of Africa is a great Ark that has, for centuries, sheltered an astonishing variety of societies. From the sophisticated cultures of the Christian highlands and the Islamic coast to the proud nomads of the Ogaden desert and the primitive tribes of the last wildernesses of the continent, the region is a true microcosm of Africa and a time capsule in which we can see many of the stages of the development of modern culture.

Inspired by deep knowledge and love of the region, this magnificent book of postcards from two of the world's outstanding photographers, Carol Beckwith and Angela Fisher, records the life-styles and customs of the women of the African Ark. Beckwith and Fisher, along with writer Graham Hancock, spent five years in the lands of the Horn recording what they learned about the native peoples, which resulted in their book *African Ark* (1990). The thirty compelling photographs included here give us a rare glimpse into the private, protected—often amazing—worlds of the women they encountered in their travels.

CAROL BECKWITH was born and educated in the United States. Since 1972 she has traveled throughout Africa, living with the Maasai of Kenya and Tanzania, and the Wodaabe of Niger. These experiences led to her two photographic books, *Maasai* (with Tepilit Ole Saitoti, 1980), which received the Annisfield-Wolf Award in Race Relations, and *Nomads of Niger* (with Marion van Offelen, 1984), which became the subject of her award-winning film, *Way of the Wodaabe* (1988). Her photographs have been exhibited and published in the United States, Europe, Japan and Africa.

ANGELA FISHER was born and educated in Australia. Since 1970 she has spent most of her time in Africa. Her first book was *Africa Adorned* (1984), the acclaimed photographic record of the jewelry and body decoration of the entire continent. She has also photographed traditional ceremonies and everyday life in Yemen, Afghanistan, Nepal, Ladakh and India. Her photographs and collections of ethnic jewelry have been exhibited in Europe, the United States, Canada, Kenya and Australia.

Women of the African Ark

ADARI GIRL, Harar

The most beautiful female adornment is often seen within the privacy of the houses of Adari families in Harar. On festive occasions, young girls are elaborately decked out in embroidered silks and gold jewelry. Their ornaments and clothing reveal the influence of designs and materials brought in for centuries from Arabia and the Far East. Local craftsmen combine their own inspirations with these imports.

Pomegranate, Box 6099, Rohnert Park, CA 94927

Women of the African Ark

MAASAI GIRL, Kenya

Beaded decorations are the most common ornaments worn by Maasai men and women. After they have completed their chores, women gather to do beadwork together.

Pomegranate, Box 6099, Rohnert Park, CA 94927

Women of the African Ark

SOMALI WOMAN, Brava, Somalia

According to the code of orthodox Islam, women must be modest in public. They are required to cover their bodies from head to toe in an all-encompassing black veil called a *bui-bui*. Despite this limitation, they have perfected the art of speaking with their eyes.

Pomegranate, Box 6099, Rohnert Park, CA 94927

WOMEN OF THE AFRICAN ARK

HAMAR WOMEN, Ethiopia

On the day after the "jumping of the bull" ceremony, Hamar women gather together, beautifully attired in their beaded skins and iron jewelry. Their hair is rubbed with fat into small balls and covered with ochre. This hairstyle is frequently set off with aluminum plaques in the shape of ducks' bills, which project dramatically from the forehead. Courtship dances follow and continue for the following two days and nights.

Pomegranate, Box 6099, Rohnert Park, CA 94927

Women of the African Ark

SURMA GIRL, Ethiopia

West of the Omo River, in a mountainous region bordering Sudan, live the Surma, who have been forced out of their ancestral homelands by the Bumi, their traditional enemies. Clay ear plugs are worn by both young girls and women for decoration.

Pomegranate, Box 6099, Rohnert Park, CA 94927

WOMEN OF THE AFRICAN ARK

SURMA GIRLS, Ethiopia

Surma girls are painted by men, especially at the time of the *donga* stick fights, when the men paint their bodies in order to emphasize their physical beauty and to intimidate their adversaries. They smear their bodies with a mixture of chalk and water and draw designs with their fingertips, exposing the dark skin in a pattern of lines. The many varying designs are largely decorative and change daily.

Pomegranate, Box 6099, Rohnert Park, CA 94927

WOMEN OF THE AFRICAN ARK

NOMAD DANCER, Somalia

From the Indian Ocean to the Somali-Ethiopian interior, nomadic festivities always include dance and song. After the rains, when milking cows are productive and the nomads are most relaxed, camel herders serenade eligible girls and impromptu dances in many different styles frequently occur. In the hinterland, women perform seductive dances using veils to the accompaniment of female drummers.

Pomegranate, Box 6099, Rohnert Park, CA 94927

WOMEN OF THE AFRICAN ARK

SOMALI WOMEN, Somalia

As a "nation" in the modern sense, the Somalis are almost unique in Africa: they speak only one language—Somali; they are further united by their common nomadic heritage, which gives a remarkable degree of consistency to their culture; and, last but by no means least, they share a single religion—Islam.

Pomegranate, Box 6099, Rohnert Park, CA 94927

WOMEN OF THE AFRICAN ARK

HIGHLAND WOMAN, Senbete market, Ethiopia

The Senbete and Bati markets are situated in foothills some 5,200 feet above the Rift valley's baking floor. Here the trade of the mountains comes down to meet the trade of the plains: on the one hand, chickens, eggs, grains, vegetables, spices, clothing and shoes—together with luxury items like soap, aluminum cooking utensils, cigarettes, tobacco and jewelry; on the other, cattle, camels, goats, sheep, part-cured hides, bars of rock salt and containers of milk and ghee (clarified butter).

Pomegranate, Box 6099, Rohnert Park, CA 94927

WOMEN OF THE AFRICAN ARK

KONSO WOMAN, Ethiopia

The Konso farmers of southwest Ethiopia grow corn, sorghum, beans and cotton throughout the year. In addition to working in the fields, a Konso woman's everyday activities include carrying firewood, grinding corn and caring for the children.

Pomegranate, Box 6099, Rohnert Park, CA 94927

Women of the African Ark

AFAR WOMAN, Rift Valley, Ethiopia

This young Afar woman is enjoying the *Kwosso* matches, one of the few large-scale social occasions that provide the opportunity for young people to strike up romantic relationships.

Pomegranate, Box 6099, Rohnert Park, CA 94927

Women of the African Ark

SWAHILI WOMAN, Lamu, Kenya

This Swahili mother, holding her child, reveals elaborate henna decorations on her hands.

Pomegranate, Box 6099, Rohnert Park, CA 94927

WOMEN OF THE AFRICAN ARK

KARO WOMAN, Lower Omo River, Ethiopia

As ochre, yellow and white paint transform the body, the spirit of the Karo is released.

Pomegranate, Box 6099, Rohnert Park, CA 94927

Women of the African Ark

HAMAR WOMAN, Ethiopia

Around their necks Hamar married women wear *esente* (torques made of iron wrapped in leather). These engagement presents, indicative of their future husbands' wealth, are made by the village smith and worn for life. An upper torque, the *bignere*, may only be worn by a man's first wife. Added at the time of marriage, its distinctive iron protrusion is both a phallic and a status symbol.

Pomegranate, Box 6099, Rohnert Park, CA 94927

Women of the African Ark

TURKANA GIRL, Kenya

The Omo River runs into Lake Turkana in Kenya. Relationships within each of the groups living in the Lower Omo valley tend to be calm, cooperative and peaceful.

Pomegranate, Box 6099, Rohnert Park, CA 94927

Women of the African Ark

RASHAIDA WEDDING PORTRAIT OF BRIDE AND GROOM, Eritrea
The Rashaida have kept in close contact with their relatives on the other side of the Red Sea, with whom they trade for the elaborate Saudi and Yemeni jewelry much favored by their womenfolk. Collecting such presents from an early age, Rashaida women are often so weighed down with ornaments by the time they marry that they can hardly move. Additional gifts are then heaped upon them as bride price or dowry. The Rashaida marry only within their own tribe and rigidly preserve their own ethnic identity.

Pomegranate, Box 6099, Rohnert Park, CA 94927

Women of the African Ark

RASHAIDA WOMEN, Eritrea

Orthodox Muslims, the Rashaida believe that women must be veiled. When a woman is married she will wear a heavy jeweled mask that reveals only her eyes. This mask, called the *Arusi*, is decorated with silver and gold and originally came from Saudi Arabia.

Pomegranate, Box 6099, Rohnert Park, CA 94927

WOMEN OF THE AFRICAN ARK

SURMA WOMAN, Ethiopia

Young Surma women are painted by men, especially at the time of the *donga* stick fights, which take place at the end of the rainy season and continue for a three-month period. Each week, chosen villages come together and the top fighters from each village challenge each other.

Pomegranate, Box 6099, Rohnert Park, CA 94927

WOMEN OF THE AFRICAN ARK

AFAR WOMAN, Rift Valley, Ethiopia

This young Afar woman sits at the entrance to a *zariba*–an enclosure made of thorny branches to deter predators at night.

Pomegranate, Box 6099, Rohnert Park, CA 94927

WOMEN OF THE AFRICAN ARK

RASHAIDA WOMAN DANCING, Eritrea

Worn from the age of five onward, a heavy cloth mask embroidered with silver threads and beads, called the *burga*, conceals a girl's form from the head to below the waist. It can only be removed in the privacy of the tent. Colorful appliqued skirts, worn in layers and heavily perfumed, like their embroidered masks, are reminders of their recent past in Arabia. Proud of their heritage, the Rashaida repeatedly call out the word "Rashaida" as they dance.

Pomegranate, Box 6099, Rohnert Park, CA 94927

WOMEN OF THE AFRICAN ARK

HAMAR WOMAN, Ethiopia

Both Hamar women and men set great store by their appearance and decorate themselves beautifully. Their bodies are well oiled and ornamented with colorful beads. Their hairstyles vary. Women tend to wear their hair in short tufts rolled in ochre and fat or in long twisted strands.

Pomegranate, Box 6099, Rohnert Park, CA 94927

Women of the African Ark

AFAR WOMEN, Rift Valley, Ethiopia

Afar virgins go bare-breasted, but after marriage they wear a shawl of transparent black cotton called *shash* or *mushal*. This is worn around the head and sometimes draped over the shoulders. Facial scarification is a means of establishing tribal identity as well as enhancing physical beauty.

Pomegranate, Box 6099, Rohnert Park, CA 94927

Women of the African Ark

OROMO WOMAN, Senbete market, Ethiopia

Oromo women are noted for their colorful headcloths and beautifully crafted silver jewelry made from Austrian Maria Theresa dollars, which were used as a trading currency in Ethiopia for many years. This coffee seller trades with the Afar at Senbete market.

Pomegranate, Box 6099, Rohnert Park, CA 94927

Women of the African Ark

KARO DANCERS, Lower Omo River, Ethiopia

Karo couples perform a rhythmic and pulsating dance, thrusting their hips one against the other in the dusty and frenetic atmosphere of early evening.

Pomegranate, Box 6099, Rohnert Park, CA 94927

Women of the African Ark

HAMAR COUPLE, Ethiopia

The Hamar pay great attention to the styling and decoration of hair. Hair styling enhances beauty and signifies status, bravery and courage.

Pomegranate, Box 6099, Rohnert Park, CA 94927

Women of the African Ark

HAMAR WOMAN, Ethiopia

Hamar married women favor a hairstyle of long, twisted strands rubbed in ochre.

Pomegranate, Box 6099, Rohnert Park, CA 94927

Women of the African Ark

AFAR GIRL, Djibouti Republic

A Muslim Afar girl from the family of the Sultan of Tadjourah is shown wearing some of the most exotic gold jewelry to be found in the Horn. Some of the jewelry is locally made and some is brought by relatives returning from Saudi Arabia, Yemen, Pakistan and India. The greatest finery is called for during marriages and other celebrations.

Pomegranate, Box 6099, Rohnert Park, CA 94927

Women of the African Ark

KARO WOMAN DANCING, Omo River, Ethiopia

Before a celebration or dance, the Karo decorate their bodies with a chalk paint. Karo women scarify their chests to beautify themselves—it is said that the skin texture of a scarified woman holds sensual appeal for men.

Pomegranate, Box 6099, Rohnert Park, CA 94927

Women of the African Ark

MUSLIM WOMAN, Eritrea

After marriage a Muslim woman replaces her heavily jeweled mask with a colorful headcloth and a black cloth covering her mouth—worn in memory of the Prophet Mohammed. (It is believed that showing a smile—a sign of happiness—would be disrespectful to the memory of the Prophet.)

Pomegranate, Box 6099, Rohnert Park, CA 94927

Women of the African Ark

OGADEN MARKET, Ethiopia

Market days in the Ogaden region create a colorful kaleidoscope of people and merchandise. Women wearing beautiful headwraps, either locally made or imported from India, arrive at the weekly market carrying goods for exchange, either on their heads or on the backs of donkeys.

Pomegranate, Box 6099, Rohnert Park, CA 94927